Heart in Pieces

A Return from Devastation

May you find hope in heart! ♡

M. E. MASTERSON

ISBN 978-1-64258-851-4 (paperback)
ISBN 978-1-64258-853-8 (hardcover)
ISBN 978-1-64258-852-1 (digital)

Copyright © 2018 by M. E. Masterson

All rights reserved. No part of this publication may be reproduced, distributed, or transmitted in any form or by any means, including photocopying, recording, or other electronic or mechanical methods without the prior written permission of the publisher. For permission requests, solicit the publisher via the address below.

Christian Faith Publishing, Inc.
832 Park Avenue
Meadville, PA 16335
www.christianfaithpublishing.com

Printed in the United States of America

In memory of my six-year-old son,
Jeffrey Raymond (November 1990–March 1997), and
my four-year-old daughter, Kaija Nicole Lomasi
(November 1992-March 1997), both killed
in a drunk driving head on collision.

Photo Credit: Mid Valley Elementary School 3686
Davis Dr. Hood River, Oregon, 97031

Contents

Acknowledgments 7
Prologue 11

Part 1

    Chapter 1 15
    Chapter 2 19
    Chapter 3 21
    Chapter 4 23
    Chapter 5 26

Part 2

    Chapter 6 31
    Chapter 7 34
    Chapter 8 36
    Chapter 9 38
    Chapter 10 40
    Chapter 11 42
    Chapter 12 45
    Chapter 13 47
    Chapter 14 50
    Chapter 15 52
    Chapter 16 54
    Chapter 17 56
    Chapter 18 59
    Chapter 19 61

Part 3
- Chapter 20 67
- Chapter 21 71
- Chapter 22 75
- Chapter 23 78
- Chapter 24 80

Part 4
- Chapter 25 83

Epilogue 87

Acknowledgments

I would like to express many thanks to my husband, best friend, and my *rock*, Mountain. Man Tom. You have had the patience of Job while I was writing this book, and I want you to know it has not gone unnoticed. The many nights of waiting for me to come to bed while I write one more thought out, only to see you have fallen asleep waiting for me. Thank you for helping me to stay focused on the most important being in our lives, God, or as I refer to him the *Man Upstairs*. It has been a long, arduous journey writing this book and I really could not have done it without either of your help. I look forward too many more adventures with you. xoxo.

My most profound gratitude and love to my dearest friend, Allison White, for sticking by my side through the good and the bad times for all these years.

To my in-laws for showing me what real loving families are supposed to be like even when things get difficult! I love you all!

To all those who took part in my journey of life, I express my greatest gratitude. These would include Dale and Linda Osgood, Kristopher White, Joe and Colette Kochis, Oliver and Barbara Schiermeister, Jerry Bowers, Dave and Vicki Weldon, Larry Hudson, Janeine Parks, Derek Nagreen, Johnny Roeder, Randy Smith, Brian Brannaman, Rob Henning, Debbie Martin and Nancy McCormick.

A special thank you to Barbara Renfro for helping me to see that my story was worth telling!

Last but not least, I am grateful to the small community and volunteer fire department of Camas Valley, Oregon for your bravery, tenderness, and love you all shared with my family and me in our time of need. May God bless you all.

I agonized over writing this book due to the personal nature in which I tell the story. All of these are memories of mine to the best of my knowledge. Some of the early years written are memories that were told to me by others who knew us at the time.

My agony entered when I was talking about assorted family members who I know will be highly upset with a lot of the stories I have told. Out of respect for these individuals, I did want to change their names, so they are not directly identified. Sadly, in our world of technology, it won't be difficult to figure out who these people are.

Due to differences in personality and religious beliefs of those family members, we have not conversed for many years, some more than ten years.

As part of my journey, I have been able to find individuals to act as surrogates for those lost family members in my life. I love these individuals as if they raised me in a loving manner that they show me every day. I will be forever grateful to them for loving me! You know who you are!

Once upon a time, isn't that how fairy tales begin?
This is a true story based on tales and experiences of my life as I remember it, a far cry from a fairy tale.

Prologue

Hope is all things to all people. No matter your creed or belief. Everybody survives on hope. Without hope, one dies a slow and agonizing death.

After losing my kids, all my hopes and dreams went into the ground with them.

Devastation like that has a way of destroying you one cell at a time.

I had always remarked that I would never live through something like that. When it happened, I wanted to disappear from the face of the earth. I had nothing left!

Christians have a belief; God will not give you more than you can handle. Well, I was definitely at my limit. In fact, I wanted nothing more to do with God himself. I even said that out loud. Anger became my function. Hope and peace had left the room!

Despair and destruction were a mission I embraced with anger. How could this happen to me? Why did I have to endure this pain? Not that I wanted someone else to have this unbearable pain. Screw Adam and Eve for not following the rules. Anger was my driving force. I was in so deep that the light could not shine through.

The pain of birthing my children was a cake walk compared to this *new* pain I was experiencing. It was as if my insides were being ripped out, rolled around in shards of glass and shoved back in my body. I just wanted to lay down and die!

Willing oneself to die takes work. The work is wearing; the time is agonizing. Maneuvering about in a *shell of mind and body* is much more comfortable. Gliding along as if you are floating, while the world speeds on by you.

God and I had an understanding; You go your way, and I will go mine. Don't need you, don't want you. Curse Satan! He can screw himself! I was told *God has a purpose* or *He needs your kids for something bigger or better.* My anger at the sound of those hollow words boiled over into a rage. God bless people who have no clue what those words mean to a grieving mother. Spilling those words out of one's mouth was like taking a scalding knife and carving it into my skin. *God needed my children more than I do,* are you for real? To hell with that! I sacrificed myself to bring them into this world. I should be able to reap the joy until my dying breath, not theirs!

I felt I had wronged *the man upstairs* so bad that he was punishing me with my worst fear. The fear of my children dying before I do. Our children are not supposed to leave this earth before us, their parents. It is not the natural order of things.

I cleaned my house of all things tied to God or religion. Zip, Zilch, Nada! Nothing left but a dumpster full!

My belief system had been finished off with the death of them both. My faith had been shattered, scattered to the winds. Now what?

I don't know if a person could be much lower than I felt the following months after they died. All I wanted was to have my babies back. To feel complete again. The reality was and is; they will never return to me in the *flesh.*

My broken self-had survived many trials. I have always claimed that a cat is not the only one with nine lives.

I struggled to figure out what my role would be now that they were not here. I have struggled with my purpose, and the answer may never come in my lifetime.

My journey would take me many places. I floundered in search of a state of belonging. I was *empty of anything worthy of giving* to anyone else. Even though I had nothing left to give, others took what was there. Stripped of all my dignity, self-worth and my give a damn, people continued to peel me down to the bone manipulating my every move to their satisfaction. I lived in a *black hole* for years!

Would I ever find the relief that I desperately needed? Would I ever find hope again? Would I ever find the much-needed peace of God?

ant 1

Chapter 1

Tuesday, March 25, 1997

I heard his keys rattle at the door of our apartment as he slowly opened it. Kenny's head was hanging low, and his face as white as a sheet. I asked him, "Why are you home early?"

I jumped out of the lazy chair I was sitting in, watching the late-night news. I grabbed the remote and turned off the television. From the expression on his face, I could see that it was something terrible. Kenny said, "I have some really horrible news about Rick and Tina."

I was instantly sick to my stomach when my intuition kicked in, the kind that only a mother can feel. I immediately went into hysterics screaming and crying back to him, "Not my babies, please God, not my babies." He tried reaching for me, but I pushed him away. He caught me before I crumpled to the floor.

Collapsed in a heap on the floor where my knees had buckled under me, I felt my life energy draining out of me. My mind was racing trying to digest this news that he has yet to finish telling me. He was cradling me while on his knees and said, "They were in a bad car accident, and nobody survived."

In my garbled hysteric-screaming cry, I demanded how he found out. He replied, "Henry called me at work."

I then sucked up my sobbing tears. I mustered up the strength to stand and break free from Kenny's hold. Frantically grabbing for the phone to call Henry, Rick's brother. I wanted to hear the news for myself. When I first tried to call him, the line was busy, so I called my best friend, Rebecca. She answered the phone. I started screaming,

"Please tell me my babies are okay." She replied crying, "I'm sorry sweetie, but I can't."

Henry had called her only a few minutes before while he was trying to reach Kenny, so she knew what had happened. We were only on the phone for a minute before I hung up to try calling Henry again.

Finally reaching Henry at his mother's house, I asked softly crying, "Henry, is it true? Please tell me that it isn't true."

He said, "It is."

I dropped the phone screaming, "Not my babies, please, God, not my babies!"

I picked up the phone again while on the floor cradled between Kenny's legs and asked to talk to my father who was there with the grieving group of family. "Hello," he said.

I replied crying, "Daddy, this hurts badly. What am I going to do? Is this for real? They can't be gone. Are you sure that Rick isn't playing a nasty joke on us?"

He said, "No, it is true, and if you had just stayed in the church (Jehovah's Witness), this might not have happened."

To which I replied with shock in my voice, "What? You didn't just say that."

In the background, I could hear my stepmother yell, "Don, No, No, No," and I hung up the phone. In my private thoughts, I was wondering if I was that bad of a daughter that he felt compelled to blame these deaths on me. Turning to look at Kenny, crying, I said, "Can you believe he just said that to me? How could anybody, especially my daddy, say such a horrible thing to me? I just found out that my kids are dead."

My body was trembling out of control, tears and emotions I had never felt before now. My heart was aching so bad that I thought it would burst right out of my chest.

After I got myself calmed down, I thought I should call my mother. I knew it would be a difficult task to talk with her because she was out in the woods on a *fire watch* (the daily routine of checking the forest for smoke or fire). She would be gone for months at a time, checking in with her neighbor periodically. I called her neighbor that would deliver messages to my mother while they were gone for the summer season. When she answered the phone, I tearfully explained that this call was an emergency for my mother. I really needed her to find my mother and have her call me back immediately. She wanted to know what kind of emergency, and I told her with a trembling voice, "My kids are dead."

She said, "I will do whatever it takes to get her out of the woods to call you back as soon as possible."

I thanked her and hung up to resume crying.

Time went by in a cloudy haze, and I heard the phone ring, which brought me back to reality. I answered the phone knowing it would be my mother on the other end of the line. She asked in an anxious tone what the matter was. I told her, "My babies are dead."

She started crying, calling out, "Oh my god, my grandbabies, CJ, my grandbabies" as her voice trailed off.

CJ, my stepfather, grabbed the phone and said, "What the hell is going on?" I told him, and he said, "Oh my god, this can't be. Are you sure?"

I said, "Yes, Dad, I am sure."

He asked, "What happened?"

I said, "They were in a car accident with Rick and Tina on their way to the coast." They asked me if I wanted them to come to my house and my reply was yes.

Kenny called Rebecca throughout the night because I was inconsolable, and he did not know what to do. Talking with her would calm me down remembering good times and funny stories. She mentioned that she was making a plan to come down to be with us. As much as I wanted her close, I did not want to put her baby in danger that was due to arrive in a couple of months. I told her not to come down, but she insisted and was on her way.

After I hung up with her, I sat on my couch and proceeded to check out of reality, not thinking, not feeling. I was numb and still in shock as if I wasn't even in the same room with Kenny. The hours dragged on before my folks showed up in the wee hours of the morning, and I was forced to check back into the real world. Upon seeing them, I broke into hysterics once again with all the flooding of feelings I had for the last few hours. They spoke with Kenny about what had happened while I resumed my position on the couch of numbness. At that moment, I could hear them talking, but it was like being in a tunnel with faint voices in the distance. I could not believe that my kids would not come through my door ever again or feel their little arms around my neck and whisper in my ear that they love me. The despair I felt was overwhelming!

Chapter 2

Wednesday, March 26, 1997

Having been up all night, all I could manage at this point was to remove my trembling, exhausted, drained, numb, and swollen-faced self from the couch to descend to the bottom of the stairs outside to smoke a cigarette and climb back to the top to return to my position on the couch. Kenny called the doctor upon my families expressed wishes for a prescription to keep me calm, so I could get through the next few days of dealing with the necessaries of burying my kids.

My mother's sister, Carey, had arrived, not sure when she did, as I was unaware of those who were coming and going. She made some phone calls into what happened in the car accident because I was never contacted personally by the state police. The police were under the impression that I was in the crash. Upon reaching the state police, they explained that an apparent drunk driver caused this accident.

On Highway 42 in central Oregon headed for Coos Bay is where the accident happened. JB had been released from work in Coos Bay a couple of hours prior. He had been working long hours for many days driving a milk delivery truck. He expressed that he needed some time off before returning to work. His supervisor gave him the following day off to go home and rest. On his way home, he stopped off for some gas and a six pack of beer for the two-hour drive home.

Rick and his family had just finished going through the wildlife safari amusement park in Winston. The kids were given carrots for a snack, and everybody snuggled in for the two-hour ride to the coast.

They planned to camp on the coast hauling their pop-up camper behind them.

About an hour into the trip, JB is noticeably swerving from line to line almost running off the road several times. He has consumed a few beers by this time (results verified in the investigation) and was falling asleep at the wheel.

Rick noticed a vehicle coming straight at him, slammed on the brakes for eighty-five feet when JB's vehicle hit them 85 percent head on, and flipped his truck over. When his truck landed, he was facing the wrong direction. When the impact happened, the camper trailer barreled forward under Rick's vehicle and punctured the gas tank causing a fire that resulted in the death of three people. However, killing both drivers on impact.

Credit: Oregon State Police Department

Chapter 3

Thursday, March 27, 1997

My aunt and mother suggested that I find an attorney to file a lawsuit. I, at first, said I didn't want to see an attorney. I felt that filing a lawsuit would only bring more heartache into this situation for all parties involved. I know how badly I was hurting and would imagine that the other sides were hurting just as much. Bringing a lawsuit up would dig up the worst, and I wasn't sure I was even ready for that. After much debate with my mother and aunt, I gave in to their way of thinking. We opened up the yellow pages and looked for the most prominent ad with the most significant amount of attorneys to handle such a case as mine. My aunt called and made the appointment for the next day.

    I, then, had to call the funeral home nearest the accident. The funeral director answered the phone. Tearfully and mildly medicated, I explained who I was. He proceeded to talk to me over the phone gingerly. He said to me that he had already heard from the other side of the family and that he had a problem that would need some clearing up. My heart dropped! He said I would need to find an attorney who could write a letter of release, so I could give him instruction on how to proceed with my children's remains. He then went on to explain gingerly, that an elder by the name of TK, from the Jehovah's Witness Church, had told him that under no circumstance was he to release their remains to me, their mother. All at the same time, I was devastated, and my blood was boiling from this new development.

I explained to the director that we had an appointment set with the attorney for the next day, and I would be sure that he received the necessary papers for their release. After I hung up the phone, I had a meltdown.

Chapter 4

Friday, March 28, 1997

I brought my divorce papers with me to the attorney's office upon his request. I was a nervous medicated wreck walking into the room because I knew I would have to spill my guts out on the table about the last few days' events. Going through all those emotions again, I was sure they would overwhelm me to the point of retreating into myself as I had frequently been doing since this happened. I knew this attorney needed me to be present to tell my story. He walked over and cupped my hand, leading me to the chair closest to him. He pulled the chair out so that I could sit. I was weeping before I could even speak. I gathered my thoughts and explained to him why I needed his services. He asked to see my divorce papers. He asked me numerous questions about how my divorce came to be. Based on what I told him, he then said that if he had been my attorney, my divorce would not have gone the route it did. I felt a sense of hope after he said that. I felt maybe I had the right attorney for the job. I thought he would fight for me, which I so desperately needed at this time. He then left the room to fax the release letter to the funeral home. Upon his return, a few words were exchanged, and we then left, headed for the funeral home.

    I don't think any parent ever dreamed that they would be burying their kids before themselves. It is an excruciating process to go through once you get past the point of accepting that they are dead. Picking out the way you want them buried, the casket or the urn you want them in, the clothes you wish to add to their charred dead bodies, the headstone style, color, sayings (epitaphs), and all the cost of doing this. Hell, I just found out they were dead, how am I supposed to do all this?

Heavily sedated with my mother by my side, we tried to figure it all out together. The funeral director handed me a book that had all the colors and styles of headstones to look through, and I was supposed to pick something out that would be perfect for them. I sat there numb, blurry-eyed trying to resist this task that I had to perform for my kids. I finally settled on a multi-colored urn as they were being cremated due to the manner in which they died. I wasn't even allowed to view them or hold them due to the conditions of their charred bodies. Then we headed off to the shopping center to pick out some clothes for them to be cremated in, it was almost Easter time.

Lion King was out at that time, and my kids loved them especially Jeffrey. So, we picked Lion King for him; For my daughter, we picked out an Easter dress or as Kaija would call it a "pretty pretty." We went back to the funeral home and dropped the clothes off along with some special little trinkets. We were told to be back in a few days, and they would have everything ready for us, meaning the urn with them in it.

I don't recall the ride home for that hour and a half. In fact, I was drained, exhausted and an empty shell at this point. The next few days were a blurry haze waiting for the phone call to pick them up.

The day came to pick up my kids' ashes. The director, who was heartbroken to the point of quitting, with tears in his eyes, handed me the beautiful urn I had picked out. He explained to me that their ashes were in separate bags and that I may find some trinkets in the ashes as they did not all melt in the process. He quickly turned and walked away leaving me standing there with what was left of my kids. I quietly wept the entire trip home for the finality of it all was sitting there in my hands.

I decided to take them to the coast to bury them in the ocean. This was the last happy place that we spent time together as a family. I wanted them to finish their trip they had started before all of this happened. I called my father to tell him what the plan was and to find out if he was coming. My stepmother answered the phone explaining that she didn't want to make that long trip to the coast. She feared that they might have the same kind of accident and then turned the phone over to my father. He explained that he couldn't make that trip. Because of their standing in the church, he didn't think it was the right thing to do as I was disfellowshipped from the church. To my father, his religious beliefs mean more to him than his family, tolerating absolutely no family member turning their heads from his beliefs.

Truthfully, I wasn't really planning on him being there anyway. I wanted him to be there more than anything, just to be my daddy for a day. I had prepared myself for this. He then, in turn, asked me if I would attend their service for Rick, Tina, and the kids. I told him under no circumstance would I be attending their services. I felt I would not have been welcomed due to my standing within the church. He then went on to say that he was asked by Rick's mother to ask me if I would give them some of the ashes from my kids to bury with Rick and Tina. They wanted to stack them on top of each other in an urn they had for them to place in the mausoleum. My response was a definite *no*! They, meaning the church and our family, stole them in life and over my dead body would they have them in death!

Chapter 5

Tuesday, April 1, 1997

Fourteen days before my twenty-seventh birthday, we headed for the coast. We left early in the morning piled in my mother's Winnebago. When we arrived on that bright sunny day, we were met with loved ones who were there to say goodbye to the kids. My brother, sister, a couple nieces, and I sang songs to the kids. A few words were said by some and then we walked down to the ocean water. My mother, stepfather, Kenny, and I walked into the water. I opened the urn to find exactly what the funeral director explained to me. I started with Jeffrey's ashes dumping them through our fingers into the waves, repeating the process with Kaija's, and returning the bags to the urn for safekeeping. Listening to the cries of others was heartbreaking while I was still numb from the inside out.

As I turned around, I noticed flowers floating in the waves. On the beach, someone had scrawled the kids' names in the sand. The scene was surreal.

We returned to the high ground where the Winnebago awaited. The sun was going down on our day. The four of us loaded up to leave. Hugs and waves goodbye were exchanged with all who attended. As the darkness approached, Kenny drove us back in silence. After everybody left our home, I really felt the loneliness set in. I felt truly alone in my own body. What was my position now? I lived my life for my kids making every decision, right or wrong, with them in mind. How was I supposed to move on from this? *Nobody understands what I am going through*, so I thought.

Emptiness overwhelmed me daily. I couldn't talk with Kenny about it as he only had *pity* to offer me, which just pissed me off most of the time. I started consuming a box of wine (cardboardeaux) daily from the time I would wake at 8:00 a.m. until I passed out around 2:00–3:00 a.m. I drank like this for three months. Kenny was concerned for my health; but with much convincing, he decided to leave me alone.

I spent a lot of my time checking out of this world while holding a glass of wine in one hand and a cigarette in the other. I essentially became a permanent fixture on the back balcony of our apartment listening to the world passing by in fast forward while I was at a standstill. I felt so disconnected from Kenny, who had no idea what was going on inside this physical self of me he saw every day. I couldn't talk to him about anything, but I could talk with Rebecca on the phone for hours. I could not perform my daily duties like washing dishes, clothes, or even going to the grocery store, which was right next door to our apartment complex. Being around people was very dangerous ground for me to be on, probably more for their safety than mine. I was a jumbled-up mess that would burst into screaming or crying at a *drop of a hat* or upon seeing small kids. I found myself stuck in a time warp as the days and weeks passed by, bouncing between the present and the past.

Part 2

Chapter 6

I arrived on Tax Day in 1970 supposedly expected to be a boy by the name of Tommy; but much to their surprise, I was a girl named after both my grandmothers who had passed.

I was two years old when my mother and my grandmother were both pregnant at the same time, due at the same time, and both were carrying boys. My mother didn't know how to feel about this surprising news, her son and her brother being the same age. When it got closer to their due dates, my grandmother gave birth to her boy in June, and my mother had her boy in July, six weeks early on both accounts. My uncle did not fare well. He had underdeveloped lungs and only lived a few days. My brother spent the next couple years in and out of the hospital with bouts of pneumonia due to underdeveloped lungs, as well.

My mother's distress of losing her brother and nearly losing her son for the same reason, caused her much heartache and pain.

When I was four, no one knew that my two-year-old brother was also deaf. We had our own little language, which got me more whippings than him because I would take the brunt of our punishments due to his inability to hear.

One night, our mother had some suspicions that there was a problem with his hearing. She looked over at me, put her fingers up to her lips, and made the shushing sound. She started sneaking up on him while he was watching television, asking him if he wanted ice cream and no reply. She continued this until she was right behind him; and, in a whisper, she asked the same question and no reply. Right then, she decided he needed to be tested. When she found out he was clinically deaf, I wonder if she reflected on those times she cracked our heads together or the many whippings she doled out. I wonder did she feel guilty for not paying attention to her children to see there was something terribly wrong. Even though we didn't comprehend what was going on with our mother, we knew she was not happy.

They admitted my brother to the hospital to have *tubes* put in his ears, so that he could hear. I believe I was thrilled and scared at the same time. Just before he went in for the surgery, he had a room with a television in it, which was turned up really loud for him. The nurse went to turn it down when he left the room for surgery, but our mother stopped her from adjusting the television; so, when he returned, he could hear the difference. When he returned later that day, he wanted the television turned back on, and he immediately screamed with pain as it was so loud; and with much surprise, realized he could hear!

Some time went by and because of my mother's unhappiness, she and my father split up. While out shopping, my mother and her girlfriend saw my mother's high school sweetheart. He pulled up in his VW bug in a one-way alleyway. While the two girlfriends were leaning in the window, a swerving Pontiac LeMans entered the alley way going the wrong way. Crushing the two women between the cars causing them to be twisted in ways a body should not have to twist. Mother had to have extensive surgery to staple and sew all her parts back together from stem to stern. In turn, she was told not to have any more children, or she would have serious problems again. After it was all said and done, the lady driving the *boat* was drinking, driving, and did not see the girls in the alleyway! My mother never spoke of what happened to her friend or if the drunk driver received punishment.

As the months passed, my parents reconciled. They soon announced that they were expecting another child. Much to the horror of her doctors who advised her not have another child, they then encouraged her to abort the child. She refused. She went in two months before the baby was supposed to be born and gave birth to a baby girl. Both had to stay at the hospital until they were healthy enough to leave. My sister was sent home with our father as our mother had to stay at the hospital for repairs. The hospital was several hundred miles away from where our grandparents, aunts, and uncles lived; so, my brother and I were sent off to live with these relatives while our mother was healing. Our aunt, our mother's younger sister and best friend, was our main caretaker at the time. She loved us as if we were her own. She was freshly married, and she hoped to have had some children of her own someday.

Chapter 7

*A*s a young child, I had a *friend* who guarded me against the cruelty I received from my parents. He protected me by *smoothing* out the hurt. I had felt His love and mercy my whole little life.

It was as if this large man was physically by my side all the time. As I reflect on this, the *man* was *God* Himself, caring for me. The love He showed me was the same love and comfort I felt from my aunt and uncle. A child wants to feel love, comfort, and security. As a five-year-old that feeling was scarce. We, as a family moved more than twenty times. We were never in one place long enough to call home. Looking back, it seemed our mother was running from something, none of us could see. Our father, committed to his marriage vows, complied with whatever his wife wanted. Despite the fact, he had to change location, church and his employment.

A month after my sister was born, we stayed the night at our grandparents' house which was not that far from our aunt and uncle's house. While there that day, our grandparents received some tragic news about their youngest daughter, our aunt. She had been killed in a house fire. Of course, we kids did not understand what had just happened as we were very young at the time. As adults, we asked what happened to her, and this is what was explained to us. Our uncle had two fuel cans next to the wood stove area to help start fires in the morning. One of the cans contained the wrong kind of fuel. When he left for work on that cold November morning, he had started the fire, but it must have not stayed lit. When she awoke to start her day, she grabbed the wrong can, applied it to the wood, lit, and it blew back in her face. The small house started on fire; and before she knew it, she was succumbed by smoke. She had tried to get out of the house, but was later found by the back door unable to make it out. She was only nineteen years old when this happened.

When the news was delivered to my parents, my mother was devastated! Despite her health, they returned home to be with her family. Things changed for the whole family, not for the best. Our father tried hard to be understanding and to show love toward his wife, but she was inconsolable. She spent most of her time depressed and unsociable. My brother and I spent a lot of time by ourselves, and when we had her attention, it was abusive. We were emotionally incapable of dealing with all the fighting and tension within the household. We cried and whined a lot which frustrated the situation further as one could imagine. Our frustrated parents would take it out on my brother and me, what they could not take out on each other.

Chapter 8

Another year passed, by now I was attending my second school. On a particular occasion, one of my classmates, the bully of the school, came to our house and told my mother that I had done something bad; and the real truth was that I really hadn't, but my mother was going to get to the bottom of it. She led me into the master bedroom and told my father to take off his belt. I was scared, trembling, and shaking while waiting for my undeserved punishment. My angry mother asked me about the information; and I told her the truth, and my mother did not believe me. She hollered to turn around, lifted her hand, and started swinging frantically with the belt. I felt the first of many swings. My legs were stinging from the belt continuously hitting my tender skin. She again asked me to tell her the truth of the information, and again I repeated what I knew as the truth.

My mother hit me again with the belt. I felt the stinging even more on top of the last lashes. This went on for what seemed an eternity—my mother was sitting in her robe that obviously she hadn't taken off all day, and my father was standing calmly behind my mother as if he had no control over the situation. When my mother became exhausted from hitting me, she proceeded to drag me in by my hair to the bathroom, where my father had just finished going to the bathroom himself. She lifted the lid and waited for the feces to flush. She forced my head into the toilet bowl; and with a washing motion, forced my head up and down in the water telling me that she would not put up with the lying. I felt as if I was going to drown. With every breath, I sucked up water through my nose and into my lungs, the burning was excruciating!

I opened my eyes, and all I could see was the inside of the toilet and water sloshing around. Was this going to be the last thing I saw before I die at the tender age of six? I had hundreds of thoughts going through my head, what was my mother thinking shoving my head into the toilet? I had absolutely no control. I attempted to gain control by grabbing the edge of the toilet with my hands and pushing up to get my breath; but the harder I pushed up, the harder my mother shoved my head deeper into the water.

Suddenly, I felt relief, my mother had stopped for an unknown reason. I lifted my head up, slowly climbed up to stand, and turned around. She was gone, and my father was standing over me apologizing over and over again in a low voice. He explained that he could not stop her, and he had no control over the situation. He turned around and left me sopping wet with my thoughts. As I looked in the mirror in the bathroom at the soaked, exhausted child, I felt ashamed! All I wanted to do was to hide forever.

Chapter 9

My father—being the subservient, passive, patient man that he was—grew tired of her unreasonable discipline of us kids, and their constant turmoil in the relationship. When the mutual decision to split was made, my mother decided to take our little sister and moved out. My mother arrived at our school that afternoon and pulled me out of my second-grade class to talk with me about what decisions had been made. She was explaining that she could not take me or my brother because she could not take care of all of us by herself. She instructed me to tell my brother, who was five at the time. She left me standing in the hallway crying hysterically while she walked away.

Now, when a divorce takes place, it is just like a death of those family members who leave. In this case, our mother had made this choice leaving us both devastated. We felt as if we were second best, not important. Thrown away like yesterday's garbage, to never see them again so we thought.

At the age of seven, I had taken over where my mother left off. I helped make dinners, did the dishes, took baths with my brother to make sure we got clean. We slept on the hide away bed together because we both had bad dreams at night; and it was comforting for both of us to be together. Our father worked long hours and had little time to spend with us kids. When my brother and I would get home from school, we would go to the babysitter or to our grandmother's house and wait for our father to get home.

In these two years, I do remember seeing my mother once. On my eighth birthday, my mother called and said she wanted to celebrate. She bought presents and a cake for me. But my father did not want her to come over because he did not celebrate birthdays, and he wasn't about to start now. He was very upset with my mother because she knew his beliefs. Not only did she leave her husband and children, but she left her religion behind, too. The church (Jehovah's Witness AKA JW) does not look kindly on leaving your family. When my mother wanted to leave, she had to go to the church elders, and they questioned her leaving. They decided to disfellowship (excommunicate) her from the church. She did not fight the decision because she wanted out.

Chapter 10

My father had grown lonely, so he sought out someone to be his companion. He found someone within the JW church, she was very young, and she fell in love with my brother and me, eventually falling in love with our father, too. But her parents had a lot to say about the relationship because she was still living in their house, and they did not want her to ruin her life marrying so young. We loved her as a mother. She was very caring and did things with us. We hoped that our father was going to marry her, but that was not going to be.

My father found another shortly thereafter in the Jehovah's Witness church. She had an abusive husband; and for her children's sake, let alone herself, she left him and filed for a divorce.

She and my father spent a lot of time together, and all their friends just knew they were going to get married. The church did not like the situation they had gotten themselves into, due to the fact, she was still legally married, therefore they were reprimanded by the church. They were forbidden to see each other until her divorce was final. You see in the church we learned from the scriptures that our virtues were sacred unto God. We were to remain pure, clean and faithful to the Lord until our wedding night. If we did not remain chaste, we then were disciplined by the church elders (chosen quorum of leaders). These elders are the father figures of the church to be respected and revered. All our lives we held their approval in the highest esteem. We were taught to trust and obey them without question.

The winter weeks went by slowly. The night that her divorce was final, my father, me, my brother, and she and her two kids went to friends' houses separately. These friends lived side by side in the same duplex. They waited impatiently watching the clock until it struck midnight, and then they ran outside to embrace each other, she was a free woman. They immediately set their wedding plans into motion. They got married at a friend's house a couple hours away because they could not get married in the church. Remember she was still, legally married when they met. She had two children, five and three, and they needed a father just as I, nine, and my brother, seven, needed a mother. When they got married, we moved over to her house and made it our home.

I wasn't sure at first how it was going to be, having her take over where I had been for two years. A new mother, brother, and sister were something I wasn't sure I wanted either, but my father was happy and that was all that mattered.

Chapter 11

When we moved in with them, I had to share a room with my new little sister which meant my last little bit of freedom and privacy was slipping away. Adjusting to this new family was not what I thought it was going to be. My father was gone longer because he had to drive farther to work; and my new mother was bossy, demanding, and strict.

With the move came a new school which was very difficult to get used to. The school was much larger, and the kids were a little friendlier, but I did not like my fourth-grade teacher. The teacher had a problem with the type of religion that my family was involved in and used that against me every chance she had. For example, Jehovah's Witnesses do not stand for the pledge of allegiance, and it seemed to me that I was the only one in the entire school that did not conform to this practice. This made for a very long and difficult half-year in my new school.

Not looking forward to returning to school, I started the fifth-grade. Much to my astonishment, my teacher became a trusted confidant and caring friend. I stayed after school frequently throughout this school year. This teacher was helping me with my math. He could see by my grades that I was really struggling. I remember on one occasion; he sat me down in his chair at his desk while he sat across the desk from me on one of ours. He was telling me that he wanted to give me a gift that was special to him for working so hard. He got up and reached across the desk, opened one of the drawers and pulled out a softball with all kinds of signatures on it. He bounces this ball in the palm of his hand, gently. Looks over at me, while explaining how this ball brought comfort and peace to him. He then proceeded to say that he wanted me to have it. I was in shock and elated! He then explained that when I play with that ball, he wanted me to have comfort and peace as he had. To this day, I have never forgotten those kinds words from my teacher nor the gift he gave me that day. In the sixth-grade, I was developing into a young woman that brought changes in me that were difficult to understand. I soon realized I was not alone in these changes. I had a classmate, a girl, who would relentlessly tease me about everything. From my body to my religious beliefs.

I arrived at home distraught one day and told my stepmother about all these difficulties with my classmate. She said she would come to the school and take care of the matter, herself. At this point, I panicked and wished I had not said anything. Because my stepmother did not hold anything back when it came to proving her point even to the point of embarrassment. My stepmother arrived at school and attended class with me asking who the girl was, and I pointed her out. At break time, my stepmother, my classmate and I all went out into the hall to have a conversation about the issues we were having. My stepmother explained that she was there to help her understand what our religion was all about. My stepmother said we loved God just like everybody else and we attended church just like everybody else, but there was one difference. Could she figure that out? My classmate said "no". So as a joke, my stepmother said, "Well do you think we are holy rollers or what?"

Oh, I could see it happening; and before I could say stop, my stepmother started demonstrating what that was. Now, she was rolling around on the floor in the hallway. I was in shock as this was not something we do, ever! My stepmother was trying to prove a point at how ridiculous this looks and who in their right mind would perform this in their church. She returned to her feet with a smile on her face and said "any more questions?" The girl turned and walked away without saying a word.

My classmate never again teased me nor did she bother me anymore. Sixth grade was a breeze after this!

The transition from grade school to middle school was all-new, as it was for everyone, that in between those stages, I wasn't sure where I fit into society. In middle school, I discovered my singing voice. Again, influenced by another teacher who enjoyed music so much that it was rare to not see him excited about music! I wanted to pursue my talent, but my parents felt that our religion took precedence. I was very disappointed, and my dreams were crushed.

Chapter 12

My parents were naturally protective of me, but probably more so because of things that had happened to me earlier in my life.

When I was seven, my father got a call from his sister, she needed to go car shopping again. Looking around in the local papers, he found a man who had used cars for sale. Upon arriving at the country car lot, they noticed it was a yard full of junk. A man appeared out of the front of this old run down farm house, he being as grey and wrinkly as the paint peeling off the house. Mr. Cunningham was wearing a long sleeved blue jean shirt with a white t-shirt underneath, smelling of stale cigarettes and cheap beer. He offered to show them the cars he had available; and without hesitation, my father and aunt followed him. While they were looking at the cars, Mr. Cunningham offered to take me off to look at the rabbits he had over across the way. I was very excited, asking all kinds of questions. How many? What colors? I could not wait to see all the rabbits.

Mr. Cunningham led me down the long line of rabbit cages to a chair sitting in the middle of the walkway. He asked me to sit on his lap. I hesitated and decided it would be all right. I was looking at the rows and rows of cages and all the different colors as it was fascinating to me. While I was admiring all the rabbits, I felt this strange hand reaching under my little shirt with these strange lips kissing my neck. As soon as I realized what was happening, I started to cry hysterically and kept asking to leave. I started to scream; and, immediately, his large hand went over my mouth and nose. He asked me to stop and promised he would let me go when I stopped on one condition that I would not say one word to my daddy or aunt, or he would kill them both. I shook my head violently, yes and he let me go. I ran as fast as I could back to my father and aunt and violently wiped my eyes, so they would not see my tears. They settled on a car they were looking at. I stayed right next to my father's leg until we left Mr. Cunningham's and did not talk about what happened for the next seven years.

Around my fourteenth birthday, my father, some friends, and I decided to go out knocking on doors to *preach the word* as they call it. We stopped at the one place I had hoped I would never see again. It was our turn to get out. I immediately started to cry hysterically, the tears overflowing, leaving my father wanting to know what was wrong. I told him that under no circumstances was I getting out at this door, and he asked why? I replied that I could not tell him or he would die. He instructed the others to go to the door while he worked to get to the bottom of this. After much convincing that if I tell him he would not die, I finally told my father the whole story of what happened to me on that day seven years prior. He was shocked to say the least and asked his friend on his return to please take us home with no explanation. It was never spoken of again in our household. A few years passed, we were reading the newspaper about a man who had disappeared. It turned out that it was Mr. Cunningham. He owned a small used car lot in town. Someone driving a Jeep Wrangler had dropped by to visit the man. Mr. Cunningham was never seen again. His wife declared him dead after seven years had passed. I remember shaking in my boots at reading this article and at the same time relieved that I would never have to see this man ever again.

Chapter 13

In my teenage years, two more kids were born into the family, I now had more responsibility. Staying up late at night when they were little to rock them to sleep, change their diapers, and generally help raise them. Looking back on my life, it was very full all the time, the schedule for the average day went as follows: wake up around 4:30 a.m. (winter), 5:30 a.m. (summer), to defrost hoses/water the horses, milk the goats, feed/water the chickens, rabbits, guinea pigs, or whatever extra we had at different times in nine years. Then go into the house and wake the kids who were going to school. Make sure they got dressed, fixed breakfast, mostly cereal sometimes eggs, make sure they had their stuff for school, and out the door to walk a quarter mile uphill to catch the bus at seven in the morning. All the while our stepmother was sleeping in her bed.

On return from school, we arrived at 4:00 p.m. to rerun the chores and eat supper at 5:30 p.m. on the dot (mind you not to be late or no supper). Then if it was church night (happened twice a week), be ready to leave by 6:30 p.m. for a 7:30 p.m. meeting, home by 9:00 or 10:00 p.m. depending on the night. Yes, I had homework, which I fit in wherever I could, many times doing my homework by flashlight late into the night. On Saturdays, during the school year, I would go knocking on doors bringing the *Good News* that we were taught to deliver. And on Sunday mornings, we were off to church again to hear the new message of hope. In the summer time, we spent a lot more time preaching the *message* that we had been taught all our lives.

With all my time occupied, I managed to find some time to go and visit my mother. Prior to this point, my brother and I had seen our mother a handful of times. The visits were usually for a week or so over summer break. Most of these trips, we traveled by bus until I could drive except for this one time.

One of the elders, TK, offered to drive us down to our mother's. He was already headed that way for a church retreat. I, personally respected this man even looked to him as a father figure. His daughter, my good friend at the time, was my age. We and our friends spent time together many times at their house. So, spending time with him was nothing new. This was important considering the length of the trip in a car together. The trip down was good but the trip back was unnerving.

On this trip back to my father's, he managed to take advantage of me, groping me, and touching me in places that he should not have been while wanting me to touch him in places I should not have. He even kissed me goodnight on the front doorstep at my father's house while my parents were in the next room. I recall my stepmother asking, "Did he just kiss you?" And I quickly denied it. I, then rushed off to my room, alone with my thoughts. I was so scared because I knew what he was doing was wrong. But I had no idea how to tell my parents. I was afraid of their reactions towards me and afraid of how the church would see this, too. This event evolved into something I could not control.

Over time, he was buying me lingerie and gifts and giving the items to me at church. I was not sure what to do because I knew that our values of being chaste were important. My morals of right and wrong were going off like a bell in my head. Yet, I was to be respectful and obedient to the elders. Nobody ever told me what I should do in a situation like this. In turn, I had to hide what was happening from everybody. I would stuff these items in my dresser drawers and deep in the closet. I was so scared that my stepmother was going to find these sinful items.

TK made sure to tell me to hide these items or we would be in trouble with our families and the church. He stressed how important it was to keep this a secret as he was one of the elders of the congregation and he did not want to be in trouble.

But it turns out, I didn't have to worry about that because he got caught one night while getting ready for church. His wife found a letter and a gift (pair of thong panties) from him, addressed to me in his briefcase. Devastated, she called my parents because she felt there was a big problem, and asked them to please look into it. My stepmother asked me if there was anything going on between me and TK. I lied and said I didn't know what she was talking about. Knowing I can't get away with lying, I broke down and explained the whole situation, including the lingerie. I was so scared!

This whole situation was brought to the church's attention and the elders, excluding TK, decided to reprimand both of us. I was put on a warning status for the church and he was disfellowshipped (excommunicated). His wife came to me to find out what exactly went on to make a decision on whether she had grounds to divorce him or not. Of course, she was devastated! This young, naïve, sixteen-year-old was molested by her husband.

Chapter 14

When I was seventeen, I accepted a job at the local grocery store in town. I befriended a guy I worked with who was four years older than me. We quickly developed a close relationship. We would take our lunches on the back of his Harley motorcycle. I was learning a newfound freedom I hadn't felt before. Always fearing my stepmother would see me or find out that I was seeing this guy. During a weekend in July, our family went to a convention for our church. All weekend, I had a hard time concentrating as I had my boyfriend at home on my mind. I had plans to see him when I got home, unknown to my parents. On my way back to my house, I made a stop by his house and spent some quality time with him, which made me very late getting back home.

My parents expected me at a certain time, and I did not make it in time. As soon as I arrived home, I knew I was probably going to be interrogated on why I was late; and despite what I tried to tell them, they did not believe me. I consented to explain to them where I was, and they were absolutely livid!

At one point, I was in a fetal position on the floor with my stepmother beating me with her fists. I was always told to respect my elders (those older than me), so I could not fight back. Then my father made me bend over the edge of their bed, with my pants down and whipped me until he got too tired to whip anymore leaving welts on the inside of my legs that did not go away for years.

My level of fear was great. What else would happen to me? Would I get beat more? I was now feeling driven to pack my things quickly. I was going somewhere, anywhere away from this terror.

Standing there with garbage bags full of my belongings, I was interrogated on where I intended to go. I had no place! I felt defeated!

My stepmother insisted on calling my boyfriend to see if she could get things straightened out. Both of my parents interrogated the poor guy for at least an hour, asking him things like, did he plan on marrying me? How was he planning on taking care of me? Did he want me to move in with him? Warning him that this was a sin. His answers were honest and clear. Hearing all of this, I was sobbing. They then handed the phone to me. My boyfriend explained that he was so sorry that I had to deal with parents like that and he apologized again, for not being able to deal with all of this. He had no intention of getting married yet. Then he hung up!

The next day, my stepmother called my work and quit my job for me without my knowledge. I was in disbelief when she told me. It was explained to me that my vehicle was parked indefinitely. And if all of this was not enough, I was then visited by one of the church elders. I was removed from my home to live with this church elders family until school break. When that came, I was shipped off to yet another church members home in another state. I felt a little bit of relief at their home even could say a little bit of freedom. They treated me like I was a human being, not a caged animal. A week or so went by; they offered me a job as long as my parents would permit me. Fear crept back in. I asked, but they refused! After a few days, I returned home with my tail between my legs. I felt trapped with no way out.

My entire senior year sucked! Despite months of being gone, I did manage to graduate, barely.

Chapter 15

From this time forward, my parents were on the hunt for a husband for me. In the winter of 1988–89, they chose one of my friends of eight years, Rick, to be a suitable mate.

My parents went to his parents and made arrangements for us to get together. We dated in the old traditional ways. We had to keep physical contact at a minimum, no making out or touchy-feely, definitely no sex before marriage. We had to have a chaperone at all times, never to be by ourselves together ever. The months passed slowly.

Rick asked my father for permission to marry me. After my father gave his blessing, Rick didn't ask me right away. He told me he had to run an errand first. He returned after a couple of hours, and I noticed he was visibly upset. He sat me down and laid his head on my lap. He told me he had just asked one of the girls from the church (daughter of TK) to marry him, and she refused. I was stunned and crushed. My heart sank, and I tried not to show him how disappointed I was that I was not his first choice. He then turned to me with tears in his eyes and asked me to marry him. I knew this was my only way out. I felt obligated to make my parents happy as they arranged this partnership, so I accepted his proposal. He handed me a bread tie for a ring just until he had the real one ready.

My parents put the family home up for sale. A couple of weeks before our wedding, they sold and bought their new home in town. I had to sleep wherever there was a bed available in the new house for the next couple weeks as there was no room for me. When my parents moved, I moved my belongings to my soon-to-be-new-home with my soon-to-be-husband.

The night before our wedding, I was told by my parents that I was to go to bed at 8:00 p.m., as we had done for years so I was fresh in the morning and not a grouch. All the while, my husband-to-be was downstairs visiting with them. The final thought I had before crying myself to sleep was, this was the last time they would ever tell me what to do and how to do it!

The following morning, I was picked up by my soon to be sister-in-law. As we left the driveway, she stopped the car and said to take one last look. And to remember that this was the last time I would ever have to go back to that place to live ever again! We, then sped off to the JW church to get ready for our wedding.

We had stayed true to our beliefs and customs, so we had permission to marry in the church. My stepmother made sure of that, even taking me to her doctor to verify I was a virgin.

With a borrowed dress, picked out by my stepmother, that had seen about a dozen brides and thirty years, I walked down the aisle on the arm of my proud and relieved father. The wedding was inexpensive, and the reception was quick. We then headed off on our honeymoon excited and nervous. Neither of us, having a clue what our future held.

Seven months later, we were pregnant. Not everyone was happy that we were having a baby. My parents came down on me hard and were quick to remind us that we are living in the *end of times*. Bringing a little one into this world was not fair. We should be concentrating on serving our God without the distractions of raising kids in these times. But for us, being pregnant was exciting. Halfway to the end of my pregnancy, I had trouble with the baby trying to come early. I was put on strict bed rest until it was safe to have the baby. I spent a lot of time in and out of the hospital with preterm labor almost losing my baby in the interim. Finally, it came time for the baby to arrive. I had some technical difficulties with giving birth, but with a snip here and there, after ten long hours, I gave birth to a healthy baby boy!

A couple days later we both were home and healthy. I was overwhelmed with the love that this little human brought to my heart. It was an incredible feeling that I knew I would never lose, and nobody could steal from me.

Chapter 16

When my son was about five or six months old, we decided to move out of town wanting to find our own way without my family breathing down our necks. So, we moved about thirty minutes away into a small mobile in a trailer park. One evening, I wasn't feeling good and was in extreme pain. We went to the emergency room, and they explained that they could not find anything wrong. Later that evening, I had a miscarriage. I was completely devastated by this development considering I had no idea I was pregnant in the first place.

We moved out of the little place shortly thereafter, moving into a little bit bigger trailer in another mobile court. We spent very little time at home. After a few months, we ended up moving back to where our families lived. We found a place for rent a couple miles from my parents, a large farmhouse on ten acres and across the street from the church. We were not real regular attenders; but now that we lived across from the church, we should have no trouble attending, so we thought. We did all right for a while; and then slowly, we started missing meetings at the church.

When I was twenty-one, I was expecting again. Once again, this was not welcome news to my parents. They felt we should not be bringing more kids into this cruel world. The *end of the world* was a phrase that we heard all our lives in the church. Bringing a child into this world was *cruel* as we did not know the time or the day when this world would come to an end. My husband and I felt very alone in our small bit of happiness.

When we found out we were having a girl; we were elated, this would be the first girl on his side of the family in many, many years.

I had complications in this pregnancy too. I was in and out of the hospital and spent many months on bed rest. When I was about to deliver this baby, I called my biological mother and invited her to be at the birth. I was very conflicted with my decision. The pressure was heavy from those around us to change my mind. She was no longer in the church (excommunicated). The bad seed in the eyes of the church. When she arrived, I had to turn my mother away after she came many miles to spend time with me. It broke my heart to do this to my mother, but I felt I was in a rock and hard place with no way out! I gave birth to our little baby girl a few weeks early. We went home healthy and happy!

Chapter 17

For years, Henry, my brother-in-law wanted to move closer to his family. We agreed to give his family the extra rooms in our house until he had his own. He had two girls who needed some positive influence, and he felt bringing them closer to his family would be just what they needed. It took a little adjustment on all our parts. My husband worked seventy hours a week while his brother did not have a job yet. He was applying to jobs but did a lot of waiting around for that job he wanted. Finally, one did come through, so he was able to purchase property and a house.

Meanwhile, I was raising kids, keeping house, and working on my cleaning business outside the home. My husband and I were not seeing each other very often. I was seeing my brother-in-law more often than my husband. Before too long, I found that I was attracted to my brother-in-law and the feeling was mutual. Over time, we eventually gave into these feelings and had an affair. I hadn't felt this alive in such a long time! I felt so conflicted because I loved my kids and husband with all my heart but cared deeply for my brother-in-law too. I could not help but feel alone at this time.

When this affair came to light, my brother-in-law and I went to my husband and explained the situation to him, so he would not hear it from anyone else. We tried to repair the damage, but I could not remain in the same town with both men there. The emotional pain was excruciating, so I decided to take off with our kids to my mother's house to take a break from the continuing situation.

A couple days later, I awoke with a start in the gut feeling that my husband was in town. My husband and his cousin showed up at my mother's place, asking for both the kids. He explained that he was missing them and wanted to visit with them for a couple hours, maybe take them to the little local exotic zoo up the way. I told him that he could take his son, but not his daughter. She was still in diapers, and I knew how he didn't like to change them. He insisted on taking both of them, without taking their car seats or diaper bag, etc. He whisked them into the car. And before I knew it I was waving goodbye and blowing kisses at my kids as they left the driveway. Time ticked on and an hour turned into two. Four hours passed and that feeling of fear crept in. They were gone for longer than he said.

He had lied to me for the first time in our life! After eight hours, I realized that he was gone. My folks and I packed up the van and headed north to find my kids. During the long eight-hour drive, my emotions and anxiety were on overload and it took a toll on me causing a migraine of all migraines. My mother reached into her purse and gave me two pills hoping it would give me some much-needed relief. We arrived in my hometown hoping to find someone who would have information about my kids, but no one would tell me anything. These were my brothers and sisters in Christ, who were not helping me in my time of need. It seemed to me that they had already marked me as an outcast. After spending the rest of the day looking for them, coming up short. My parents dropped me off at my marital house. I decided he would return at some point, and I would be there to get my kids back. After breaking the door down, because the locks had been changed, I entered the home. I hadn't had any sleep in twenty-six hours and was so terribly sad. I decided I needed to get some rest. They headed back to their home.

My thoughts were running rampant with questions like how did my life change so drastically? Where are my kids?! He worked so fast in getting things planned in three short days, how does that happen? Who else was helping him? The church elders? Our church friends? Our family members? God, why was this happening to me? Trying to calm my emotions, I decided to have some whiskey. I went to the freezer where we kept it and drank it hard and fast! When I finally woke, I was met with people telling me what I had to do next and my friend telling me everything will be alright. She said she was very happy to see me awake after they had to restart my heart. I then passed out again. When I woke again, my friend explained to me the only way that I could go anywhere, because of accusations of my attempt at committing suicide, was to go to the mental ward. The ER then released me. My friend drove the hour to drop me off at the mental ward. I remember nothing of the drive or the check-in. The next day, I woke up in a padded room in a hospital gown not knowing how I got there. Three weeks later, I walked out of the hospital with orders to see a therapist hoping to see my kids, but instead was met by my brother-in-law with divorce papers in hand from my husband. I was devastated!

My husband ended up with custody of the kids, and I ended up with open visitation and paying child support. Again, I was devastated! The church had managed to get their fingers in our lives once more. They had actually helped him kidnap our kids from my mother's house. They had helped him switch vehicles in our hometown and advised him to stay in a motel across the state-line. I was labeled unstable due to my forced visit to the mental ward and as I found out later, having possession of the kids is nine-tenths of the law.

As a result of this affair, I lost everything! First, I lost my self-respect and my pure relationship with my husband whom I had grown to love like I thought I should. Second, I had marred my relationship with my God, and my relationship with the church (I was removed from the church). Thirdly, I lost custody of my kids in the divorce, and everybody that knew me turned their backs to me wherever I went. I was an outcast!

Chapter 18

I stayed in our hometown even though it was very difficult for me. After a few months of living with my brother-in-law, I moved out of his place into my brother's little RV. I was labeled as homeless by the state and forced to collect food stamps so I could survive. I tried to find a job, but our town was not very forgiving especially after all the rumors and gossip. I looked for months and finally found one in the fall. A tourist who had recently moved to town and bought a restaurant, gave me a chance after I had tearfully begged him for the job. I walked ten miles daily for this minimum wage job, but I did not complain. I was very grateful.

I did get to see my kids whenever I wanted. The courts had ordered me to pay $50 for child support. Rick and I agreed instead of cash that I would buy the kids winter gear. Any extra monies I could manage to save would go to food for them while they visited me while I literally, starved. On my days off, my ex would drop off the kids for me to watch saving on babysitting costs for him, and I got to spend quality time with my kids. I would get so angry at him for referring to me as the babysitter. I would tell him over and over that no matter his thoughts it did not change the fact that I was and always will be their mother.

After a period, I moved from that tiny RV to my brother's place. His apartment was a one bedroom that he was sharing with another guy, so it was tight. Before I moved into this space, his roommate who was nineteen, and I, twenty-four, had become intimate, so we decided to share his space in the living room.

We fell hard for each other, and after a few months we were talking marriage he even went as far as to buy me a ring. During our relationship, I learned that as a teenager, he was in trouble with the law. He admitted to me that he had molested some of his younger family members. He was removed from his family and ended up in an adolescent home for troubled kids. I was angry when I first heard this news wondering why he let me fall in love with him. Then my next thoughts went to my kids, and would he do this to them? He promised me that he would never, and I believed him because I truly loved this young man.

Somewhere in the middle of this relationship, I met my best friend, we were like sisters. My boyfriend was working with this guy that he befriended, and they thought it would be great if their girls could meet, so they made a plan. When we arrived at their humble abode, I immediately recognized his wife. After a bit of time visiting, we put the pieces together; her mother was one of my babysitters when I was younger. She and her twin sister would relentlessly tease my brother and me. While visiting with her, I was introduced to her friend. We *clicked* right away, all three of us talking all through the rest of the day, and were pretty much attached to the hip for months.

My new best friend was graduating from High School, and she wanted to live closer to town. So, we decided, along with my boyfriend, that we would all get an apartment together across the river from my hometown. We found one that suited all our needs and moved in right away. Her parents were not altogether sure that they wanted us associating together, let alone living together. But they eventually warmed up to me many years later.

As the months passed, I came to realize that I did not want to strap him with my mess. We were going two different directions, so we ended it.

Chapter 19

After my breakup I went back to the one thing I found security in, singing. My nieces and I wanted to start a singing group. I was introduced to a new world that I had no clue about. We would hang with other troubled young people (an official gang, so it turned out) who had nothing better to do than to cause trouble. I, along with my best friend and my nieces, dove in with both feet. I became their protector when trouble presented itself. We were a gang inside the bigger gang. We stayed up until all hours of the night, partied on until dawn, and slept our way to the top, so we thought.

All of this came to a screeching halt for me after a girl we knew, by the name of Anna, was murdered. From the stories I heard, this is the best I can recollect. Anna was continually bullied by a gang girl. She, Anna, tried hard to be friends with this gang girl but this person was cruel and vicious to her. She would go home crying to her mother many times after school. This gang girl wanted to be rid of this nuisance, so she came up with a plan. The gang girl gathered the other gangs to have a party and invited Anna to attend. The party was just up the street from Anna's house so she did not have far to go.

During the party, the guys and girls started harassing and humiliating her. Then one of the guys pulled out a gun telling her that they were going to kill her. She got up to leave, and one of the guys shot her in the head. The sound of the gun emptied the house in a quick hurry, and the gang girl ran off to her house to tell her father what happened knowing that this had gotten out control. The guys, who had taped this whole event, in the meantime, had taken Anna and stuffed her in the trunk of their car because they were sure they had killed her. Unbeknownst to them, she was still alive, barely. When the police found her, they immediately had her flown to a hospital that could deal with a gunshot to the head. She later died from her injuries.

We, girls, were scared more when we found out more information on what really happened. I personally felt somewhat responsible as I was not there to protect this innocent girl. We went down to her mother's house to see if there was anything we could do to help her out. Little did we know the District Attorney was looking to find us to see what we knew. When they contacted us, we really did not want to be involved; they even used her mother to talk to us. She was convincing, but we were really scared for our lives. The DA went as far as to put us up in a local motel so that we could feel safe. I never did say a word about anything I knew, which I don't believe was much anyhow. My knowledge was all based on rumor.

All this time, I was extremely concerned for my kids, all of these *bad* people knew my kids, and I was sure they knew where they lived. Although I was concerned for my kids, I never once said a word to my ex-husband about this trouble that I felt I was in.

Somewhere in this mess of a life I created, I met someone from my past. This man was a brother-in-law to my old church friend. I met up with him one night, and he took me to his house. He first forced me onto his bed and assaulted me tried to rape me, but could not make things rise for the occasion. He then forced me on to the couch while shoving his man parts into my mouth and finished his business. He then asked me to get cleaned up; and if I ever told anyone about this incident, I would pay so would my kids. I spent hours in the shower after this incident. I called my old church friend to explain what her brother-in-law had done. She was in disbelief. She explained that she could not and would not believe me. I can only assume she brought it to his attention because he later threatened me, through my brother. He said he would kill my family and me if I ever accused him of rape. If my friend didn't believe me, who would?

My survival instinct kicked into gear I picked up my proverbial bootstraps and went about looking for a job. If I was going to get myself out alive, I needed to save some money and move out of town altogether. While working there, I met another man who was straight as an arrow when it came to his life direction. We came from similar backgrounds, country people, raised by strict protective parents, and both looking for a new life away from this stigma that was placed upon us. Defying all the rules of our job, we started seeing each other, and eventually moved in together into a small one-bedroom apartment. At first, we were able to hide our relationship from management, but after a few months, the rumors got around to the store manager. We were forced to make a hard decision, quit working together or quit seeing each other. We decided that I would quit my job and to start looking for a new store for him to transfer to.

One came up with a transfer, so we packed up. We found an apartment about a mile from work. I decided to apply at this new retail store while I explained to them that we were seeing each other, it would not be a problem for us to work together. They made arrangements for us to not be in a position where he was my boss in any form, it worked out nicely. I excelled at my new position in this store and was in a management position within the week of being on the floor. Our relationship developed over the next year into an engagement, and we were planning on having a late spring wedding the following year.

Between my job and planning our wedding, I was under a ton of stress. All this stress was taking a toll on my body, it literally decided amongst itself to shut down. It was slow at first, but came to a complete shut down after a few weeks. He took me to the emergency room quite a few times to see what was wrong with me. I couldn't even go to the bathroom by myself, feed myself, or talk straight for that matter.

After seeing a neurologist for three months, we were no closer to an answer to my plight. The doctor sent me off to a university hospital to see a better specialist who might be able to give us some answers. I walked into the doctor's office in this large hospital facility. He asked me some questions and directed me to go down the hall to see somebody else and then come back and see him. So off I went to this other doctor who turned out to be my answer after many months of none. He gave me two cortisone shots in my shoulder muscles; and almost instantly, I could feel relief. I wanted to go out dancing! I thanked him for his help and went back to the other doctor to hear what he had to say. He explained to me that I had muscles that got tight and were not going to let go until they had some help.

While this was happening, the blood was not getting to my brain properly, which meant that the basilar artery to my brain had non-repairable damage. He explained to me that I need to keep stress free, participate in swimming, exercise, massage, and have chiropractic therapy, preferably for the rest of my living days. My response to him was if he would like to adopt me, I would be pleased to participate in all of these activities for the rest of my days. And with that, we left his office to never return. I did get the chiropractic therapy and massage for a while after this visit, which helped a lot.

We continued to make plans for our upcoming wedding. We visited every weekend, sometimes had my kids along, at his family farm a couple hours south of where we lived at the time.

I spoke with my ex about getting the kids in April. I was looking forward to seeing them on my son's kindergarten spring break. But before I got the opportunity, a drunk driver took them all on the evening of March 25, 1997.

Part 3

Chapter 20

After the accident and all the people were gone, I decided to clean house in the sense of a spring type cleaning. My anger drove me to clean out anything spiritual or religious related. I felt if God was all-powerful and could save my kids, then how come he didn't? Was my earthly father, right? Was this punishment for me from past sins of long ago? If I deserved such a terrible heartache like this, then why could he not have taken my life and let them live? Could someone please answer this question? That was all I wanted. They suffered such a tremendous death, why on earth would such a loving God put them through that? Why not save them? With my heart ripped in two, I did not get any answers that satisfied my questions. So, in return, I was eradicating Him from my life for good. I did not want to have anything to do with such a being as this. *How cruel can One be?* so I thought.

I started with all the bibles that were in the house then moved on to books, magazines, trinkets, furniture, clothes, linens, and anything else that made sense at the time filling a couple dumpsters. Included in this purge was anything that was given to me by my father and stepmother, pointed directly at her, mostly. She had such a hold on my father from the beginning that he wouldn't stand up for himself. He was always leaving the issue in her hands to handle, and it showed. She wears the pants in the family if you know what I mean. The father I knew once upon a time would never have said the things he had, nor deny me, of being my daddy. I ended with a final goodbye with my middle finger pointed straight up to the heavens. I no longer wanted *anything* from Him! Our apartment was empty!

In June, Kenny decided we needed to make a change in location taking me out of the city and into the country. We packed up what we had left and moved to his parent's house until we found a place of our own. He transferred his employment to the nearest facility. I, was not sure if I could handle a job with people, so I took a break for the summer. I was going through detox from drinking so much over the last few months too. His parents, being the kind, good Christian country folk who don't drink a drop nor do they partake in anything that may be unhealthy such as tobacco, would not put up with a drunk in their basement. I soaked in the country air every chance I got and spent my time trying to figure things out.

One morning, shortly after we arrived, I woke screaming out loud, which scared Kenny and his parents to death. I explained to him in my dreamy state that it was all a joke, the kids were still alive. Rick brought the kids to me in my dream, so that I could see them. They were not gone after all! I started to jump out of bed, and Kenny grabbed me by the shoulders and yelled at me to calm down and listen to him. He said, "I am sorry, but your kids are gone. We buried them, remember? It was just a dream it was all a dream."

I broke down in hysterics and cried for the rest of the day my heart breaking all over again. This dream I had went something like this, Rick had Kaija in his arms with Jeffrey standing on his left side appearing on a country road walking toward me explaining to me that he had something to say to me that was really important. I replied "What?" in a hushed tone because I was so stunned to see them. He said, "I am here to say I am sorry for the way I treated you all this time."

He did not realize how much pain he had put me through and was truly sorry for everything. And he came back to give me a chance to say good-bye to our kids. We then started walking down this country road, now with me holding Jeffrey and Kaija's hand.

We walked past this cyclone fence that had a stack of flowers as high as the fence. It was in front of two stones in a cemetery. I was curious but wanted to keep going to see where we were headed. At this point, Rick veered off to see this linoleum factory leaving the kids with me. We, the kids and me, wondered off to find grandmother as she had a gift for the kids. She wanted the kids to have a pig to take back with them. I explained to her that they couldn't take this pig with them. She argued with me for a bit, and then the kids were gone again. I told her I had to find them. I went about searching for them in this little town that looked like a place you might see in Finland or Switzerland.

The doors were short, and the buildings were small. I looked down the street to find Rick, and the kids exiting one of those buildings. They had ice cream cones in their hands, eating them happily, and Rick tells them to wave to Mommy. "We have to go now." With waves good-bye, kisses were blown, I love you's were said, and they were gone.

As the days passed, I could not get this dream out of my mind. I eventually concluded that it was so visual that it had to be true. Rick had come to me to apologize for the last few years of heartache that he had a part in. In turn, this was the start of my healing. I was still very angry with God, waking every morning cussing him the first thing while others were praising him. I would continue this for years to come as a daily practice.

I did seek out others like myself to talk to because I needed to understand my feelings. I was desperate to find answers about my grief. Was it normal to feel the way I do? Why do others react the way they do? Would the feelings of despair, emptiness, and loneliness ever go away? Would I ever quit crying? Would I ever be the same again? Kenny's mother understood where I was coming from but did not feel comfortable talking about her loss or her feelings. So, I felt I needed to seek out somebody, anybody who could help me. I found a group called Compassionate Friends. This group is directed to help bereaved parents. I was extremely apprehensive about sharing my grief with others. Had any others lost more than one child? Had any other lost their only children? Losing one was excruciating but two, there are no words to describe that pain. I found it very difficult in a group setting and was told that there was a group online that might be more my style. My young twenty-seven-year-old mind, connected to this way better.

Kenny continued to work to support us eventually getting a place to rent. I tried to make our house our home, but I was so empty that I no longer had anything to give to anyone, let alone the man I was supposed to marry. I decided that I had to move on from this glass box, I felt he kept me in. I loved him so much that I had to let him go.

After a tragic event happens like this to a person, *time* is irrelevant. Days pass into months into years; and before you know it, when you awake from your stupor, you have no idea how you got to where you're at and when you got there.

Chapter 21

Eventually, I moved from here and there, in and out of relationships with men for years, drinking and smoking until I passed out only to wake to do it all again the next day. I really had no feelings left for anyone else, let alone myself. I felt like a shell of a person with no direction or purpose, way beyond empty. I didn't care what my place was in the rat race of mankind, why should I care? God didn't. Nor did I care what He thought anyhow.

I bounced in and out of my biological mother's house appearing for a moment, and then I would disappear once again, this time into the arms of a man with three kids. I stayed there for about a year and a half, and we split.

Not long after that, I fell into the arms of yet another man, Eric, whom I married a week after I met him. This husband would be my wake-up call. He introduced me to the Wiccan ways of his life, which I grabbed on to like a life raft to the spiritual realm. I learned about my inner self and started to heal from the tragedy that was drowning my whole self. I realized that I was still a mother, and I was still a person who had feelings; and, most importantly, a person who wanted to live.

Eric brought out these feelings in me by being the person he was, which was controversial, contradictory, and abusive at times. With Eric, it was his way or the highway no ifs, ands, or buts about it. Most of our lives together, I spent walking on eggshells, so I wouldn't get the subtle abuses he threw my way. For example, three weeks after we were married, we were traveling down a Kentucky highway going seventy-five miles an hour in an eighteen-wheeler while he is yelling at me, pushing me against the door, and telling me that I needed to get out of his truck because I was way to sarcastic for his liking.

I replied with a smile on my face that I wasn't leaving while the truck was traveling down the highway at seventy-five miles an hour; and that if he wanted to stop, I will get out and be glad to get another ride with another trucker. He stopped pushing on me and told me to shut my mouth not to utter another word for the night. I obliged. It was at that moment I realized I wanted to live! I did really care about my life, and I would be damned if he was the one that was going to take me out.

After almost five years, Eric and I made the final plunge of divorce. I moved to my friend's place in another state while Eric continued to harass me. We continued a dysfunctional relationship for a few months after our divorce until I finally said goodbye.

My relationship with my biological mother continued to be rocky at best. She and my stepfather had many financial hardships. They had to sell their property to get them out of hock. They moved about the country in their RV, not lasting in one place long enough to call home. They eventually moved in with her other sister and live-in boyfriend. After months of living with them, my aunt calls me up to see if maybe I could help find a way to get my folks some land to live on and out of their house. I wasn't sure how this was going to happen, but I was open to the idea. After talking to an attorney, I found that for a price, I could pull some monies out of my annuity that I had from the kid's wrongful death suit. I moved forward with this plan, I told my aunt's boyfriend that I would agree to go forward as long as I would be able to pay off all my current debt. My aunt's boyfriend agreed to co-sign on a loan for a piece of property because I had no credit to borrow with being freshly divorced. We found a twenty-acre piece with a house, shop, and barns right in our price range. I moved forward with the purchase, despite the warnings thrown my way from my friends. They were concerned for my well-being, going into a business deal that included my biological mother. How would this go with both of us living on the same property? Well, I had a lot of wishful thinking on my part and brushed it off, thinking it would be just fine.

The time came to sign my name on the dotted line. I hesitated because the amount to put down on the property was not what I agreed upon; but with a lot of nudging from my aunt and her boyfriend, I relented. I also was taking a beating on my personal income to make this deal happen, losing 70 percent of my monthly income for ten years to draw monies out early. I moved forward despite my hesitations and signed the papers.

Now, I was locked into a large loan payment that my monthly income barely covered. I would have a place to live and so would my mother and stepfather, so I thought. A few months passed, and my mother said that she talked to her sister's boyfriend, and they felt it was high time that I move off the place and go live my life. Get a job, get a boyfriend, or whatever I wanted to do, but go nonetheless. I was shocked! You did what? Why?

I had paid for half of this property (down payment), and the other half we split 60/40, my biological mother paying 40% to her sister's boyfriend in the form of rent. Then, behind my back no less, they wanted me to move off the property and get the life they thought I wanted! I had the life I wanted! I was working my butt off every day to take care of the property, which was now full of horses we had rescued over the last few months.

I flipped out and screamed back at my mother saying this was my home now just like hers, and I was not leaving! She then told me that I had exactly until midnight to get my stuff off the property because I needed to go get a job. She explained to me that she could not afford to keep paying for my half of the electric (which wasn't much because I wasn't using all that much living in their forty-foot travel trailer, I gave them my house to live in), my part on the grocery bill (I gave them what I had left for groceries which wasn't much I admit), and the monies for the feed bill for thirty horses (mostly came from donations). In exchange, we had previously agreed that I would work on the farm to feed, clean, fix fences, clean stalls, and took care of sick and injured horses.

I continued to say, what more could she want from me? Her name was not on anything, what right did she have telling me to leave? She then informed me that her sister's boyfriend wants me to leave too. Wow! I was in tears, again my mother has told me she doesn't want me! I turned to her and screamed I wish she would die! A few moments later, I was threatened with a shotgun by my stepfather to leave the property. I called my attorney and was advised for the safety of my life that I should call the sheriff and leave the premises until this issue could be resolved. With help from some friends, I packed and moved off the property to never return again. I filed a lawsuit to recover the money I gave towards the property. Three years later, it was settled out of court. The property was trashed which brought the value down to bare minimum. The house required a ton of money to repair the damage that was done, so the house sold as is. The land was empty and overgrown. I never recovered all the monies from this deal. I was relieved when the seller papers were signed. I haven't talked to any of them since 2006. It cost me too much.

Chapter 22

After I was forced off my property, I moved closer to my friends. I moved into my friend's house. They were having troubles of their own with their marriage, which pushed me even harder to find a place of my own. In this very small town, not much came available as far as rentals were concerned; but through a friend of a friend, eventually, I got my own place, an apartment all of five hundred square feet, quiet, in the woods, and out away from people. I had a couple of boyfriends in between that didn't amount to anything but heartache. I found some work a few miles from my apartment to give me something to do and make a little extra money.

I did a lot of soul searching, mind you I still was waking up every day and cussing out God. My kids were always in the forefront of my brain when I was by myself, which usually ended in me being a slobbering drunk making calls to people who I am sure were tired of hearing me crying on the phone about my kids. One morning, I found myself half dressed in the bathtub with vomit and diarrhea all over the place. It took me a few minutes to realize where I was and to make out what had happened.

I decided then, that it was time to clean up my act, or I was going to die! I told myself that I didn't want to have to face my kids and explain to them why I wasn't where I was supposed to be because I had died drinking. I scrubbed the place down and decided that I needed to make a change, to what I wasn't exactly sure. About this time period, my very good friends showed up at my little place and offered their home to me. They said they would give me a job, which meant learning a new trade, and I could have the downstairs of their place (two thousand square feet) rent free! My reply was I would have to think about it. My pride stepped in and said you don't need their help.

A few weeks passed, I quit my job, gave notice on my apartment. I took them up on their offer to move into my new living quarters with a job attached, understanding that I would do this for a year then reevaluate the situation. I was eager to learn something new and to be around new people who didn't know me or my past. I struggled with my drinking for some time yet, but I did not let myself get slobbering drunk as I had before. I had to be responsible and accountable for my actions or I could lose all of this new life. I spent my off time with horses, so the loneliness wouldn't swallow me up as it had done in the recent past. My friends had horses, so we would go riding together, and this kept the ugliness at bay, most days. My friendship with them also turned my head back to a more positive direction of living.

Here I am, ten years after the accident, still trying to figure out what my role was in life. Was I still to label myself a mother? I didn't have any physical bodies to prove that I was a mother. I had plenty of stretch marks on my belly to prove I had given birth to babies, but how would I prove it to others? Anybody can have pictures; anybody can make up a story, but who would want to? Any real sane individual wouldn't want to tell this story! I decided it really didn't matter, it did happen, and I didn't need to prove anything to anybody. They were dead and not here in the physical realm, and that was that! So, my role was a working single person who lost everything, and everybody that I ever loved. I spent a lot of time figuring out if I was worth loving or could be loved again. What was love anyhow? My father loved me on conditions, if I stayed in the religion, if I did what he told me to do, he loved me. It was his way or the highway.

My mother loved me on conditions, if I did things her way or manipulated a situation to her gain, or if my money paid her way, she loved me. My stepmother loved me on conditions, help with the raising of my siblings, cleaning the house, doing my chores, never talking back, and the list goes on and on, she loved me. My first husband was "in love" with someone else entirely, only after her rejection did he grow to love me in our arranged marriage. My second husband, who had been raised by the state, was unfamiliar with the concept altogether. So, what was true love anyhow? The only time I ever felt true unconditional love was from my kids. They shared that love with me freely and openly as most kids do with their parents.

My friends brought me into a whole new world that I hadn't experienced before. They cared about me as if I was one of their family members. Living in their home, I learned how others lived, how others truly treated each other, and how people loved one another despite their own hardships they were enduring. Leo was a survivor of cancer only given a 10 percent chance of surviving and living proof that nothing could get in his way of living life to the fullest. Jane was battling depression and always searching for a way to get back into the light of life to enjoy it with her husband. And they both showed me what true love of a marriage was all about. They both showed me that I was worth loving, and that they truly cared about me and my well-being. I felt their love for me as if I was their daughter, not a special project. I look back at this time with great fondness.

Chapter 23

Leo shared with me that he had attended college all those years back to become a minister. He asked me if I had ever thought about pursuing a relationship with God again. I refused to have any conversation with him about God whatsoever. In fact, I explained to him that God, and I had an understanding that involved me giving him a piece of my mind every day. Leo said he could see why I would feel that way, but would remind me that God has never left me and will be there when I am ready to come back to Him. Bull huckey! No way in God's green earth did He ever want me back! After all I had done and said in my life would God want me back, ever, I wasn't worth it! Even my earthly father had told me at one time that I would never have God in my life after I was kicked out of his church. I was a sinner; and, therefore, God would not love me because I had turned my back on Him. I didn't see that I was worth loving, so why would God love me? Leo never gave up on me when it came to God. In passing, he would tell me that God loved me, and He was just waiting for me to come back.

Leo's conversations stirred up memories of my past relationship with my heavenly Father. As a young child, I talked with Him as if he was standing right next to me. Remembering Him with fondness when He would tell me what a good little girl I was and that He loved me. Remembering the Other Man (Satan) who was mean to me with words that only hurt me for years by telling me what a naughty little girl I was. My heavenly Father always stepped in to try to guard me from those hurtful words. I always felt growing up that I had a close relationship with my heavenly Father. I never worried about my physical needs even as a teenager with secular responsibilities. He always took care of me; but, in turn, I relied on Him with all my being. It was considerably different now so many years later.

About ten months in to this new life, this particular morning, I woke with a stirring in myself that I hadn't felt before. I was so tired of being angry to the point of exhaustion for the last decade, that right then and there I made a conscious decision to get on my hands and knees in my living room while raising my hands toward the heavens and said out loud, "You win! I am so tired of being angry please take this from me, please forgive me for being so angry with You cussing you out every day and help me to move forward in a way that is pleasing only to You." I, at that moment, felt like a huge weight had been lifted from my shoulders of burden and I bawled like a baby until I fell asleep once again.

One of my friends gave me a Bible as a gift, and I began reading it once again. It felt like foreign ground at first, but soon became like an old friend who welcomed me back with open arms.

It was weird to read another version (KJV) of the Bible as the one I was familiar with was from the religion of my youth. I eventually acquired a taste to explore other versions, as well as the one I was most familiar with, to compare, so that I was getting an unbiased message. I would pray, which took some practice at first because I hadn't prayed in so many years, that God would help me to get the message he wanted me to learn at that time.

I was by no means consistent in reading or praying for that matter. I had to play this mental game with myself to remember that I asked for God to be in my life now, I had to take responsibility once again and be accountable in everything I did. I had to reteach myself that I was not living just for me anymore, I was living for God. This took years to learn, but I have a purpose, I have a role in life. I belong! I learned that God loved me, I am his child, and nothing I could do would ever make Him abandon me. I was the one who left Him for a period and He was a God of forgiveness. All He ever wanted from me is to Love Him and worship Him, and He would take care of me. I am His family!

Chapter 24

After living with Leo and Jane for a year, I decided to move on. I moved to Iowa for yet another man. We went through a flood in 2008 that almost wiped me out of all my earthly possessions, which in itself was quite devastating. Moving was not a foreign ground to me; in fact, in my growing up years, infant to seven years of age, my parents—prior to their divorce—had moved more than thirty times most likely due to my mother's unhappiness. I had gotten pretty good at packing, only taking what was really important and leaving the unimportant behind. My Missouri friends, who I had known since my second marriage, had an extra house to rent. We accepted their offer to move into their extra house although we did not last long. He went back home on a bus.

I met yet another man who I shared time with for a bit. He introduced me to the author, Eckhart Tolle, who had a different look on life. While reading his books, I learned that my kids' death did not have to be my identity, which is something that I used as my life definition. I felt a relief in reading that my life could be different in how I think and act. Giving myself permission to not feel guilty about moving forward. I was and am still a mother by definition, and that my life doesn't have to be doom and gloom because of this terrible tragedy that I experienced. That it was all right to be happy; and it was all right to move forward, in fact, imperative to my survival in this journey of life.

Part 4

Chapter 25

March 2009

So I did! While creating new friendships online, I found a Montana man, fondly called Mountain Man, who was, in my opinion, very intriguing. I, at this point, was in a *time out* period when it came to intimate relationships. You could say I was really exhausted by the *game*. I was learning to cope with being *alone*, but keeping myself busy, so I wasn't lonely. We started talking online, passing emails back and forth, and talking about Eckhart Tolle's book, *the Power of Now,* and the Bible. We talked about goals in our life, our pasts, and our futures. The subject of my kids did come up in conversation. I wanted him to understand that the baggage I carry is heavy and deep. I am not always an easy person to live with. Explaining how difficult living this life can be. He in return explained that he didn't have any children and wasn't planning on having any.

With the months passing by, we realized that our kinship had blossomed into something more. While there were many miles between us, we decided that we would like to pursue a more intimate relationship. A few months passed, and he came down to help me move up to Montana. We married a year and a half later while his parents were on a visit.

We have in depth conversations about God and what He has in store for us. Using prayer on a daily basis trying to figure out what we are supposed to be doing for Him. We try to keep faith and trust in God in the forefront of our minds.

Mountain Man and I were discussing forgiveness one day. He explained to me that in order for me to move on from this I would have to forgive those who have trespassed against me. And I also needed to forgive myself. I read the scripture based on Matthew 6:14–15, "For if you forgive men when they sin against you, your heavenly Father will also forgive you. But if you do not forgive men their sins, your Father will not forgive your sins."

I held a grudge toward JB for killing my family and up to this point, I really didn't want to let this go for fear that I would become complacent toward the memory of my kids.

I asked God almost begging him to help me to forgive this man, JB, and to help me to forgive those who had taken advantage of my situation for their own greed. To forgive those family members that denied me of their love. To forgive myself for the guilt and shame I felt toward my kids. "If we confess our sins, He is faithful and just and will forgive us our sins and purify us from all unrighteousness" (1 John 1:9). Saying it out loud was really uncomfortable at first, but it was a relief beyond words. I truly felt in my heart that I could forgive JB, but I never will forget what his actions did to all the families involved.

I look at my first forty years and wonder how in the world I made it thus far? And, in reality, the only way I have made it is God's Grace. *The Man Upstairs* has put up with a lot from me. He has shown me that forgiveness is an ongoing process, and His love is forever.

Picture owned by Masterson

Epilogue

In closing, there have been many lessons I have learned in my life. The one that has stayed with me the longest is not everybody has experienced loss of any kind, especially losing someone close to them. Therefore, not everybody can relate to those feelings that come with the loss of a loved one or two.

Not everyone is raised in the same manner as the next kid. The family that lives life with love, structure, and freedom of life has no clue what another has gone through with abuse, brainwashing, manipulation, abandonment, and lots of tragedy. On the same hand, I cannot relate to their life that I only dreamed of. I can try, but will never truly understand it. Not everybody has drama in their life, nor do they need it or thrive on it.

Love is not on conditions. The Bible in 1 Corinthians 13:4–5 says, "**Love** is patient, **love** is kind. It does not envy, it does not boast, it is not proud. It does not dishonor others, it is not self-seeking, it is not easily angered, it keeps no record of wrongs." I was raised to understand that love had conditions, if I did this or that, Daddy would love me. If I did not follow his religious lifestyle, he would disown me. And my mother loved me as long as she could manipulate and control the situation and relationship we lived. Love never fails! In my recollection, *true love* does not fail. One cannot love another if they do not love themselves.

The biggest lesson I have learned, God is forgiving. All he really wants from us is that we appreciate everything He has done and continues to do for us. That He truly loves us even though we continue to foul up our lives despite even our best effort to make it right according to His will; and that despite all my *cursing him* all those years, He was still there for me in the end. I can look back and see where He was protecting me, despite the hurt and ache I carried for so many years. Even to this day, He is still keeping me safe and directing me in my faith.

Speaking of faith, He has taught me that faith in Him is always what keeps us on the *yellow brick* road. Learning to trust Him was one of the hardest lessons I had to learn. That means letting go of my will and being patient to wait on Him to get all the little pieces lined up for what He wants me to do, which sometimes is really difficult. Looking for direction from Him in all aspects of my life. Faith and trust go hand-in-hand. He heals all and will take care of those who are hurting if one just lets Him heal their heart. Letting God take the pain from us is part of the healing process. Hanging onto it only gets one closer to the six-foot hole that awaits us all.

Because of this experience I have also learned that my kids are not too far from me. Remember the dream I spoke about, with Rick and the kids coming to me. Well, I have had much more since then with my kids in them. They stop to say hello to their momma which brings me great comfort. All through the years, the kids have used two mourning doves as their symbol for letting me know they are watching over me. I know that I know, they are not far from me at all times. When I run into new people, they are curious about where I come from and how my life journey brought me to where I am today. And the one question that is usually asked is, "Do you have any kids or children?" Now, I always hesitate in answering this question, not because I don't know the answer, but because I have to decide right then and there whether I want to get into the details of my past by saying yes, or just pass over it by saying no.

Most people do not know how to respond to death, let alone when you explain to them that it was your kids who died. A child dying is a subject that will forever be touchy. They aren't supposed to leave early, but the truth of the matter is, it happens every day everywhere to somebody. Most times, I dive in with both feet because I want people to know that my kids' lives were not for nothing. I feel a person should say their names, Jeffrey and Kaija, so one does not forget those precious lives, which someone carelessly took from us.

    I tell my story so others can learn from me; and I tell their story so others may learn from them.

If you find yourself in need of talking to someone over the death of a child/children, please contact:
Compassionate Friends Organization Toll-Free (877) 969-0010
https://www.compassionatefriends.org/
Jeffrey and Kaija's memorial page– https://victimsofadrunkdriver.blogspot.com/
My personal blog page – https://adventures--of--life.blogspot.com/

About the Author

M. E. Masterson makes her home in Missouri with her husband, Mountain Man Tom, in a peaceful little holler fondly called Ozark Serenity Acres.

Photo credit: Photoloco Photography 2906 Decidely St. Green Cove Springs, Florida, 32043

CPSIA information can be obtained
at www.ICGtesting.com
Printed in the USA
FSHW02n0822300518
48611FS